SHADES OF LOVE
THE NAKED TRUTH

Poetry From the Soul
To Heal the Soul

Written and Illustrated by:
Rose-Ann Robinson

SHADES OF LOVE - THE NAKED TRUTH
Written and Illustrated by Rose-Ann Robinson

Published by:
SpiritWorld Publishing
P.O. Box 1447
Bloomfield, NJ 07003-1447
info@spiritworldpublishing.com
www.spiritworldpublishing.com

© Copyright 2006 by Rose-Ann Robinson
© Illustrations copyright 2006 by Rose-Ann Robinson
ISBN # 0-9779739-0-5

Library of Congress Cataloging-In-Publication Data

This book was printed in the United States of America

ACKNOWLEDGMENTS

I want to first and foremost give thanks to **GOD** my Father who has guided my hand and has made all of this possible even when I thought it was impossible.

An extra special thanks to:
My wonderful mother **Ms. Sonia Gordon**, my number one fan who has always believed in my dreams. My beautiful sister **Ms. Melinda Robinson** for being one of my biggest supporters. **Mrs. Romelia Jones** who always told me she knows *I have a love for words.* **Dr. Sharon Lewis** who always told me to *keep writing.* **Mr. David Gittens** for being a good friend and advisor.

The following people have played a very important role in my writing career by believing in me. They have also helped to uplift my life in their own way. Thanks for always being there for me in times of need and for just being who you are:
Samoya Bailey, Sherwin Bascomb, Karen Birchak, Edward Black, Kiamue Boniface, Andre Brown, Gordon Brown, Grace Brown, Lauren Brown, Samantha Brown, Tafari Brown, Kashon Burden, Devene Burke, Dorian Butcher, Denise Campbell, Fona Campbell, Ohan Carty, Tony Culture, Michael Dorman, Janet Douglas, Rosaline Downswell, Dr. Wandolyn Enix, Ryan Foote, Destiny Gittens, Carol Gordon, Keith Gordon, Leroy Gordon, Shawna Grant, Nicole Hearon, Gayle Henderson, Kanene Henry, Cynthia Hunter, Joan Hutchinson, Joy Ismajloski, Adela Joyce, Ivan Lee, Nancy Lomax, Rodney Long, Daphne Mahan, Garnet Marcial, Byron McIntyre, Marc Medley, Sophia Moncrieffe, Copeland Myrie, Dameon Myrie, Ericia Myrie, Rayon Myrie, Selina Nelson, Maurice Oates, Andrew Parkes, Louis Phillips, Miesha Pierce, Viveen Pinnock, Mary Prendergast, Kelvin Quince, Janice Reid, Sandra Rexach, Melanie Richards, Evelyn Richardson, Norris Rochelle, Marcia Rodney, Shawn Rodney, Steve Rodney, Kim Rose, Antoinette Sadler, Brianna Sadler, Rebecca Simmons, Patrick Simms, Kathy Skeetes, Pastor Dr. David B. Thornton, Tom Ursetti, Carmel S. Victor, Jane Warren, Leston Welsh, Jeff Wiley, Ericka Williams, Nadine Williams, Uhia Willis, Lovena Wilson, John Zablocki, and all others who have touched my life in their own special way.

In Loving Memory Of:

Eric Gordon my loving grandpa, the best friend God could have ever given me.

Mr. Michael Godfrey a friend who always encouraged me to pursue my writing career.

Ms. Minetta Wright a wonderful friend who embraced me as one of her own children.

Thanks And I Love You All!!!

TABLE OF CONTENTS

~♥~

CHAPTER 1 – LOVE, Hello, Falling In Love, Bliss

CHAPTER 2 – YEARNING, Hunger, Wanting, Needing

FORWARD

Each selection in *SHADES OF LOVE - THE NAKED TRUTH* captures the essence of the many facets of love. Every chapter speaks to the beauty and in some cases the pain of having loved, lost and loved again. I have always found writing to be extremely therapeutic and in creating each poem, found myself coming closer and closer to the truth.

I truly believe that *SHADES OF LOVE – THE NAKED TRUTH* is beautifully and soulfully written and it is my intent for the reader to experience a familiarity with each situation that will ultimately create an intimacy between the reader and me. I look to educate those who've never been in my shoes and comfort those who have. All of the sketches are originals by me and are included to strengthen the overall feelings of the related chapter.

Many friends tell me that I am using God's gift of writing to help readers feel as though I am their voice, speaking for, through or about things they yearn to say aloud, yet remain silent. I have been writing for several years and have in many instances experienced what I am sharing with you. Perhaps it is these experiences that allow the poetry to touch you in such a deep and special way.

I would love to hear how *SHADES OF LOVE – THE NAKED TRUTH* touches you. Feel free to email me at <u>rrobinson@spiritworldpublishing.com</u> to share your experiences with me. Until then, never give up on the most powerful force in the world, which is love.

****** Look out for Rose-Ann's upcoming novel summer 2007! ******

DEDICATION

This book is dedicated to every man and woman who has ever felt the most powerful and incredible force in the universe......*LOVE.*

LOVE

BITTEN

Have you ever been bitten

Have you ever been touched

Have you ever been enlightened

By the spirit of love

Have you ever felt the fire

It's a blessing from above

It's an exciting experience

The feeling of love

APPRECIATION

'Tis the time to show appreciation

To the person that I love

It's the time to give adoration

To that someone blessed from above

Your caring thoughts

And loving heart

Can help me move

Even mountains apart

With all my love

Dedication too

I extend this feeling

I'm in love with you

♥-♥-♥-♥-♥-♥-♥

THE DAY WE MET

From the first day I met you
I misread your style
We exchanged our emotions
Without even the slightest utterance of a word

Your eyes told me, you didn't want just to say hi
But instead, to become my close companion
My heart skipped a beat
And then it happened again!
Just then I wanted to run over and speak to you

Rushed from accepted but misinterpreted sensations
I wanted to walk over to you and say hi
But my pride kept away a privilege
One undefiled

The privilege that once could have been wasted
Assumedly one that wouldn't now be in existence
If I had never seen you
But I guess I was too scared

I was scared from the passion in my heart
Scared from the flames I saw in your eyes
Where would I be now?

Would I have been
In an impenetrable void
In a land lost without the feel
Of having never been in this form of forbidden lust

I marvel at the thought of my having never before met you
Oh the fool I would have been
To pass up one as passionate
Caring
Charming
Sensual
And as breathtaking as you

BROWN SKIN GUY

Hey you

You

Yeah I'm talking to you

The one with the dark brown eyes

You see

I've been watching you for a while

You have been playing on my mind

Temptation sets in

Every time I look at you

And your breath-taking smile

Has me feeling for you

You keep my mind always working

With that perfect cute smile

You have my heart forever racing

At an hour per mile

WHEN I LOOK AT YOU

When I look at you

I feel like I'm in a dream

I fantasize about being with you

I think about you and me

When I look at you

Your eyes seem to always speak to me

They tell me to come a little closer

To fall right in a dream

When I look at you

Your lips, they smile at me

They tell me to run right over

To continue my fantasy

When I look at you

I see you and me

When I look at you

I continue to feel free

When I look at you

Whenever I look at you

When I…

Look at you

MAGNIFIED

Whenever I see you

I see your lips

I see them shining

I see them smiling

I see them glistening without a cause

Whenever I see you

I see your walk

It seems to always

Be in my view

It's the sexiest thing I find in a man

Whenever I see you

I see your chocolate ebony skin

I see the smoothness in your tone

It seems to glow wherever you go

I like your dark cool complexion

Whenever I see you

I see your firm broad shoulders

I see the manliness inside of you

I see the every evidence of your mere existence

It's like a puzzle with all the clues

LOVE IS

My baby you know just what love is
For when you touch me I can feel it
My baby you know just what love is
And I can feel it in your every kiss

The sun seems to shine brighter
When you look in my eyes
The world seems a lot warmer
When you're smiling with me

Everyone seems to be happier
All possibilities seem nearer
Friends are all in alignment
Families seem to be totally in sync

The future becomes more probable
Dreams are the in thing
Understandings are more popular
Fantasies become real

My baby you know what love is
I see it every time I look in your eyes
You always seem to keep my temperature on high
That's the way you always make me feel

ONE MOMENT

At the moment I saw your eyes,

I felt tension between my thighs.

I sensed you had a rise,

From your ever enormous size.

As you pulled me towards you,

I could see that you knew.

That we both didn't have a clue,

Of this feeling that's brand new.

Then you put out a grin,

Inside I wanted to sing.

As you touched my skin,

You had my mind out of sync.

♥◆♥◆♥◆♥◆♥

I'LL SHOW YOU HOW

Said you wanted a poem
So I'm gonna write you one
Say you wanna get to know me
I'll try to show you how

Be true and honest and caring
Stay calm cool and collected
Keep doing the good you're doing
And I'll show you how

Don't ever stop being charming
Try never to lose that smile
Stick around for a while
And I'll show you how

Be aggressive yet gentle
Continue that same slick style
Keep that spark in your eyes
And I'll show you how

Stay smart hopeful and peaceful
Treat others as you'd have them treat you
Be forever positive
And I'll show you how

Don't ever change who you are
But continue to work on your flaws
Try not to ever stop living
And I'll show you how

There you have your poem
You've inspired me to write these lines
Stay humble and forgiving
And I'll show you how

YOU

It's great to have you near me

It's great to have you around

You're a person I'm sure I can talk to

All year round

You bring joy and happiness to my life

You're a delight to be around

You make everything seem simple

You're the talk of the town

I've never met anyone like you

No one quite so profound

You've got charm and charisma

You never wear a frown

Don't ever lose that passion

Don't ever let it die down

That's what you've always told me

You deserve no less than a crown

FORBIDDEN LUST

You bring out something in me

That I know should not be there

I get butterflies in my stomach

Whenever you give me that stare

I don't know if you're feeling it

But I'm sure something's there

Maybe I'm the only one feeling it

From all the moments we've shared

FORBIDDEN

Now is the time in life

When I can truly say I've fallen in love

The unfortunate thing about it is

I cannot share it with anyone

My situation is so complex

I do not even know where to begin

It's funny that the greatest thing that could ever happen to anyone

Is now happening to me

Only to find that because of his situation and mine

We are unable to let the whole world know how we feel

We've never both felt this way before

It's scary, risky and exciting at the same time

We want to share it with the whole world

But because our love is forbidden

We must hide our feelings for each other

We dare not say anything to anyone

Because of this, we are afraid of getting each other hurt

I'm crying out inside

Because this is the one time in my life

When I can really say I'm in love

The scary part for me

Is that I have no questions as to whether I do love him or not

I must keep my mouth closed

Because no one would believe me

AWAY SONG

Take me away
To that beautiful place
Where the sun is always shining

Sing me a song
In that beautiful place
Where the sun is always beaming

I tried my best
I tried my best
To show you how much I really love you

Pull me apart
Pull my heart apart
And see the things I'd really give to you

I needed you
Needed a man
To show him how much I do believe in him

I cried no tear
I cried no tear
Because God knows how much I do trust in Him

Trust in Him, trust in Him, trust in Him
You better do believe in Him
That's God

So take me away
To that beautiful place
Where the sun is always shining

♪♥♪♥♪♥♫♪♥♪♥♪♥♪

YEARNING

I YEARN FOR YOU

Every beat of my heart
Hungers for your touch
Hoping I could get
Some of that loving
I want ever so much

I whisper your name
Hoping you'd hear and rush on over
Telling me you feel the same
While showing me that you couldn't care less
Of what may happen next

I want you to press
Your hard bod' against mine
Sharing this energy
Which seems to be without end
One which cannot be denied

Show me how blessed you are
And I'll give you a part of me
That has never been shared with anyone
Cause only our Creator could understand
How much I'm burning up inside for you

My patience is running thin
And I cannot hold back this sensational
Heart throbbing experience
Which is causing me to put this pen to paper
Exploring all the possibilities which only words
And emotions can see, feel and take in

What is this hungry
Heart stopping
Climatic excitement
And forever
Anticipation I'm feeling inside

Just come and take me in your arms
And show me how a real man is…
Supposed to make a true woman feel
Kiss and caress me
Let me breathe
Help me to ease this tension going on inside
Lay me down and take me
To the highest of all highs

SITTING HERE

I'm sitting here feeling lonely
I'm sitting here feeling blue
Sitting here wondering if you'll call
Not knowing what to do

Why do I continue to put myself
Through this pain and suffering
Why do I keep making myself feel used
Why do I allow myself to experience all these tragedies
Why can't I see the clues

I'm sitting here feeling lonely
I'm sitting here feeling blue
Sitting here wondering if you'll call
Not knowing what to do

Thank God for a good night's rest through sleeping
Thank God for all his views
Thank God for giving me strength and vigor
For I really haven't got a clue

I'm sitting here feeling lonely
I'm sitting here feeling blue
Sitting here wondering if you'll call
Not knowing what to do

Being patient is what I'm trying
Though I'm running out of fuel
Being patient is all I have left
Cause I don't know what else to do

I'm sitting here feeling lonely
I'm sitting here feeling blue
Sitting here wondering if you'll call
Not knowing what to do

Be careful cause I'm falling
Be careful you know it's you
Be careful because I'm crying
Boy you've got me so confused

I'm sitting here feeling lonely
I'm sitting here feeling blue
Sitting here wondering if you'll call
Not knowing what to do

LOVE SICK

Love sick

I guess I am a little love sick

I'm missing you so much

Maybe a little bit too much

Every ounce of my body

Wants to be with you so much

My love

How can I show you

That I desire your touch

Your clutch

The mere way you make me feel

I just got to have you so much

Is there a way for me

To escape these pains

From the longing I get

When I'm awaiting your touch

Help me to get another taste

Of your forever loving touch

DEAR LOVE

I can't stop thinking about you
No matter how hard I try
My heart is filled with tender care
And sometimes I want to cry

I always think of you holding me
Especially when I want you near
My heart feels like breaking
And I feel a great feeling of fear

I wonder what you are doing
I wonder if you do care
I wonder if you'll need me
For your heart I want to share

I always try to call you
But you are never there
Do you ever feel for me?
Because I surely hope you care

I don't know when I will see you
I wonder every day
The longing I have for you
No man can ever compare

If I ever do see you
I hardly really care
Cause the shock I get of seeing you
Makes me so very scared

When you start to show me love
It makes me feel
That I've been blessed from above

If you ever decide on leaving me
I won't be mad
I won't start crying
But I surely will be sad

Until then Love…

DON'T FAKE IT

Even though you keep running

I know you still love me

Even though you keep hiding

I know you still want me

You try your best just to fight it

But inside I know you're crying

So maybe you should just try to face it

For inside you can't shake it

I DREAM OF YOU

I often dream of you
Holding me
Kissing me
Caressing me
Pleasing me
Teasing me
Completing me
While keeping me
Wrapped up with the thought of feeling you

I'm glad to be your queen
Your delight
Your breath of fresh air
With a bright ray of sunlight
You're my ocean breeze
My constant tease
My angel with a sling
My melody when I sing
You're my American King

I always think of you
Wanting you
Taunting you
Haunting you
Flaunting you
Calling you
Falling for you
While seeing you
Wrapped up with the thought of being with you

♥♪♥♪♥♪♥♪♥♪♥♪♥

TO NOT BE ABLE

To not be able to talk to you

To not be able to speak to you

The tortured feeling I often get

Just to not be able to be with you

To not be able to sing with you

And I can't get to live with you

I won't be able to laugh with you

Still I can't even walk with you

To not be able to breathe with you

And I can't be able to be in your shoe

You can't be able to be in mine too

All the pain it creates just to be without you

I wish another day

Together we'll be again

I wish that some day

Again we'll be holding hands

I wish on that day

We will be more than just friends

I wish on that day

Together we'll be till the end

MISS YOU

I am missing you

I am missing you my baby

I'm wishing you were here with me

Cause I'm needing you my baby

I know that you still care for me

Cause I can often feel your pain

The rain keeps falling down my face

The clouds barely seem clear

The sky stays dark when you're not here

The birds they don't seem to sing

Since you went away that hurtful day

My life has taken a spin

My heart skips a beat

Whenever I think of you

And this pain I feel inside my heart

It's forever crying out for you

It's been a while since I last saw you

It's been a while since we've said we're through

It's been a while since we had that feud

It's been such a while…right now I am through

MY LOVE

The more I fight you
The stronger you become
The less I fight
Your weakness I see

The more I resist calling you
The harder it becomes for me
The longer I don't speak to you
My weakness you'll see

Everyday feels like ten years
And every hour feels like a week
And every moment I spend without you
Seem closer to eternity

My love for you though I never did say
My love becomes more and more real
My love I'll share until the end
My love's only for you and me

●♥●₪♦₪♥●₪♥₪♦♥₪●♥●

CONVERSATION

Temptation to pick up the phone to call you
As I hunger to hear your voice
I crave to hear you speak to me once again
Just one more time

If only I could get another chance to speak to you
Just once again
I would be in total glee
Hearing your voice is like music to my ears

It's like angels singing, in an attempt to promote peace
My baby when I hear you speak to me, it puts me in a state of mind,
Of total peace and total contentment

My heart jumps around, and my tone remains in a high and exciting volume
Then my voice would go back down into a soft and melodious tone
Only to show how warm and humble you make me feel

While a calm comes over me and takes full control
It's as though God has taken over
I hardly wonder what move you'll make next
I just freeze in the moment
Hoping our conversation on the phone, would never come to an end

DRAGGING ON

Pains from temptation
Tears of frustration
Cries from contemplation
Weeps beyond this nation

Singing for jubilation
Shouts for salvation
Screams for purification
Joys beyond this nation

Praying through separation
Meditating on situation
Fasting for realization
Praising beyond this nation

Believing in relaxation
Hoping for celebration
Seeking rejuvenation
Faith beyond this nation

Freedom from tribulation
Wisdom through motivation
Kingdom of specialization
Blessings beyond this nation

BREATHE

Breathe in

Breathe out

The dizziness is about to set in

The shortness of my breath

And the constant chest pains

The hurt in my stomach

The fluttering of my heart

It's continued skipping of beats

And the trembling of my hands

The repeated pep talks

And the calming of the nerves

The holding back from crying

And the sobbing from the nose

So breathe in

Then breathe out

I'll keep the rhythm a flow

That's the strategy

My best measure

My most effective fighting tool

PARALYSIS

It's like a balloon about to pop on my inside

A burning which takes away my breath

A fire running through my arms

The effect of electric energy causing my fingers to go numb

That's how I feel every time you call

And every time I hear your voice

It drives me crazy

My heart continues to skip every other beat

My air passage becomes smaller

My chest expands and becomes lighter

I take deep breaths to refill

Then the burning continues through my legs

It feels like it would never end

It feels like an eternity

The cycle of the never ending pain

It seems to always go on and on and on…

~♥♪♥♪♥♪♥♪♥♪♥♪♥♪♥~

ENTRAPMENT

How do I explain it
When all I feel is entrapment
It's like being stuck behind walls
And being unable to find a way out

How can I share with you
The feeling of discontent
The numbing on the inside
And the cold sweats on my forehead

How can I show you
How hard it is to be vulnerable
I'm always thinking about you
I constantly watch the phone

Every time when I eat
I can't seem to taste a thing
All I do is just swallow
Reality barely syncs in

If I scream
Will it make any difference?
Will someone hear me?
Would anyone comprehend?

WHAT'S IN A TEAR

Memories of sheer laughter

Memories of security

Memories of tranquility

Memories of being your queen

Memories of you and me

Memories of hope and peace

Memories of joy and pain

Memories of a beautiful summer's day

Memories when you feel sick

Memories of pure conflicts

Memories of special days

Memories of a love unsaved

What's in a tear

These are the ingredients

Combine them all together

They'll bring you sad times

But also a future filled with happiness

CLING ON

Waves of uneasiness
Slivers through my stomach
As a surge of electric current
Runs up and down my spine

Rolls of pain
Are defined
As knots of tension
Are in design

A time for longing
And a time for pain
A time for releasing
And a time to show gain

There's a place in my heart
That holds on to you
There's a place in my smile
Crying out for you

Every move that I make
From the steps that I take
I try hardest to shake
What these feelings create

No matter the struggle
I'm still open to love
Though time is a battle
I'll cling on like a glove

HELL

Another day in hell

Another day going through these fiery pits of hell

Someone save me from this madness

All this craziness and stupidity

Which consumes me to the point

Where it's almost controlling my whole being

Remove me from this torture

Lord save me from this rain

Lord quench my thirst, my desires

And relinquish all this pain

CONFUSION

Robinson 9.16.02

ENLIGHTEN ME

Take me for a ride
Help me to see the whole show
Help me to see the things
You already know

How can I be there
If you're already gone
Your body might be here
But your mind is all wrong

You tell me you need me
Say you're going through hell
Say you're hoping I'll comfort you
But I can't even tell

Say you're trying to get to know me
Say you're thinking it through
But you're caught up in your own world
You leave me sad and blue

I get pains in my stomach
And tears in my eyes
I try my best to understand you
But to me it's all lies

HOLD MY HAND

I want you to help me understand
What you're going through
I have never been in your shoes before
Therefore I cannot empathize with you
But I can try my best to sympathize
With what you're going through

Don't shut me out
For I haven't even gotten a chance
To know you
Help me to see and feel your pain
Your heartaches and strife

Take me into your world
Show me what you're about
Don't close the door
Before I even get a chance to step in

I'm hanging over a ledge
Latching on to a piece of string
I'm hoping that you'll lean over
And grab a hold of my hand

Stop trying to seem so perfect
I know we all have flaws
Just hold my hand I'll walk with you
Who cares if we get lost

To be lost with you
Is what I dream
I enjoy every moment with you
Being lost with you inside a dream
Is definitely what I'll do

DON'T KNOW IF IT'S WRONG

I'll sing you a song

Don't know where I belong

Are my feelings for you wrong

Don't know if it's wrong

Don't know if it's wrong

Don't tell me it's wrong

Just sing me a song

Don't know if it's wrong

Where do I belong

Is it in singing your song

Just where do I belong

Don't know if it's wrong

Are my feelings for you wrong

Shall I sing you this song

Don't tell me it's wrong

Don't know if it's wrong

Don't know if it's wrong

Try singing me a song

Don't know where I belong

Don't know if it's wrong

WHAT COULD THIS MEAN

What could be happening
What could this be
What could be his motive
Where could he be

I wonder if he's in hiding
I wonder if it's a game
Is he really being serious
Or is he just lighting my flame

Could I possibly get an answer
Lord show me a way
Will I be left crying
Pretending I was caught in the rain

Is he real serious
When he say's he's taking it slow
Is he really taking it easy
When he doesn't even show

I asked about him phoning
He said it must be his mind
He forgets how to function
When he's dealing with my kind

Women are from Venus
Men are from Mars
Should that make much of a difference
When we've gone this far

STUPID

If only they knew

That he's been wishing and praying

While I've been stopping and blocking

As he waits for something to happen

What kind of woman do they think I am?

Do they think I'm some kind of a floozy?

Who's out wanting a doosey

I am a woman of class

Not looking for something fast

For that which would never last

In life there's a primary cast

But through Christ

Only through Christ

This too shall surely pass

∫♥♥∫▲♥∫♥♥∫▲♥∫

THEY DON'T KNOW

They said it should be easy to be me

But no one really knows who I am

No one knows the pain and sorrows I feel

They don't know what it's really like to be me

But you're so cute, is what they say

You shouldn't have a problem finding a man

You probably have to pick and choose each day

I say, you don't know what it's really like to be me

Days ago I've seen happiness

Others were filled with tears

It's ludicrous to predict what my future holds

They just don't know what it's really like to be me

Many a nights I've cried to sleep

Other nights I stay busy

My friends all tell me I seem satisfied

But, they don't know what it's really like to be me

Is there a solution to this problem

I guess time will only see

I thank God for giving me strength

Cause, they don't know what it's really like to be me

I AM MAN

I don't need a woman…

I need the perfect woman
To come around
So I can mess things up
Then start all over again

That way people will see
That it's not me
It's these crazy women
They have in this society

Then the woman will also see
That the joy of being with me
Is simply a fantasy
She was only living a dream

How can anyone believe
That things could be so perfect
There wasn't even a time
When it wasn't really worth it

The relationship was working
But someone must have cursed it
I really tried to fix it
But it was doomed from the get go

Tell all those crazy women
To come sign up and join the show
My values don't seem to be working
Starting over's the way to go

YOU'RE THE BEST

You're beautiful

You're perfect

You're exactly what I've been looking for

Now I've got something to tell you

You're not exactly what I expected

So I'm writing just to tell you

Goodbye

A MAN NOT YET READY

I've got something to tell you….

I've been looking for a woman,

Just like you.

I've asked God for someone brilliant,

Someone like you.

But until I met you,

I realized I'm not ready for you.

I'm not yet ready,

I just ain't ready,

For someone as terrific as you.

TO YOU FROM ME

I gave you me
And it was all for free
I felt so unclean
And you continued to be so mean

One night of pleasure for you
A night filled with pain for me
I thought you said you loved me
But it must have been in my head

I really do love you
And I always will
My heart will always crumble for you
And the feelings shall remain still

I've cried many tears
And I've had sleepless nights
I thought I was your woman
For you were my man

I'm still in love with you
But I cannot trust you
Tell me something new
Because I haven't gotten a clue

Is there another woman
Or is it that life you love so much
I can't see how you could forget me
Cause I did feel love in our touch

HE'S CONFUSED

This isn't working
We don't see eye to eye
Let's be friends
Now I'm gonna bang my head against the wall

I can't talk to you
I don't know what to say to you
I'm dumbstruck when we're on the phone

Okay let me write a letter
You're great but I just can't be with you
We just differ on an important issue

I'm gonna still try to stick around
And shower you with gifts
But no don't take this as a weakness

I'm gonna be in your life
But not the way you want me to
Just sit back and let me do what I must do
Okay bye now

I just came by for a short visit
I don't know when I'll see you
So try not asking
I'll call you when I feel like it

Don't you dare pick up that phone
I'll be the one to contact you
For I'm not sure what I'm doing

Hi it's me how you doing?
Okay I'm finished talking to you
Later when I feel like it
I'll call you once again

No no why are you so jolly?
I still need time to get over you
You don't understand what I'm saying
I need time to get over you

46

Hi it's me are you busy?
Is there something the matter with you?
You should be happy to hear me calling
Don't you know I'm the one with the views.

Oh what's wrong with her?
Didn't she know that it was me?
Is she crazy is she insane?
She should be happy hearing from me

Hi baby it's me again
How you doing I hope fine?
I was calling but can't tell you
My real reason for your time

It's great to hear your voice
You must be busy I could see
What was that?
No you've got things confused
I am not ready to restart things

That's not the road I want to take
At least not so very soon
I'll put it again in writing
So you can see I had you fooled

Don't go I'm not finished talking
You have no knowledge what I'll do
I'm sitting here and also wondering
I don't even have a clue

♠♦♥♠♦♥♠♦♥♠♦♥♠♦♥♠♦♥♠♦♥♠♦♥♠♦♥♠♦♥♠

PUSHED

Have you ever felt so burdened?

As if someone was sitting on your shoulder

Pushing you and pushing you

As though you'd go right in the ground

Have you ever felt inflated?

Where you feel as though you can't go on anymore

There's something that's tugging and pulling you

As though you'd explode into the unknown

Have you ever felt so annoyed?

As though no one else understands you

You feel pressured and jaded

It's as though you'd run right out of town

Have you ever felt frustrated?

Where you just want to forget it all, everything

You feel mentally abused and totally used

You just want to scream out loud

Have you ever felt so mistrusted?

As if you have no purpose for existence

You've been watched and clocked just like a crook

It's as if they want to turn you into a clown

MY MAN

When I see him with her,

It makes my heart bleed.

Anger consumes my body,

Frustration gets the best of me.

If looks could kill,

She would have already exploded.

For the way I feel,

Only God He knows it.

Everything I do,

She tries to walk in my shoes.

Everywhere I go,

She tries to follow my flow.

Every smile I make,

She tries to capture its taste.

Every friend I make,

She tries to pull them away.

Why can't she just leave me,

Let me be at peace with who I am.

It's funny I've been her teacher,

Now she's trying to take away my man.

WHICH ONE

Which one of us do you really love?

Which one do you want it to be?

Which one of us do you care about?

Which one do you want it to be?

Which one of us makes you smile some more?

Which one makes you very happy?

Which one of us gets you emotional?

Which one do you want it to be?

Which one of us are you always thinking about?

Which one keeps you laughing?

With which one do you want to share your love?

Which one do you want it to be?

I've driven around

And walked all about

While wondering if it's me

I've set my sails

To head out of this jail

It shouldn't matter if it's even me

MAN STEALER

Man stealer

How did you come to be so mean?

Man stealer

Come out and make yourself clean

Man Stealer

Why did you have to choose him?

Man stealer

What did I ever do to make you cheat?

You look in my eyes

And smile in my face

You tell me we're friends

Which indeed you're not

You're a traitor I believe

You can never be trusted

You're a liar, a cheater

One who'll someday get busted

EGG SHELLS

You're always ignoring me

Telling me I like to complain too much

You tell me I have a problem with everything

Saying I put up too much of a fuss

Whenever I try to talk to you

It's as though I'm walking on egg shells

You act as if I'm not there

I may as well be talking to myself

There were times you were kind to me

There were times you made me feel good

There were times you had me smiling

And there're times you made me feel new

I keep myself around you

Even though I constantly feel used

There're times you have me wondering

Is this the situation I wanna choose

HE'S BACK

He's here

He's back

Now I'm confused

I really don't know which one to choose

I met him last year

The other I met him last week

The one last year

I called him my king

One I had been sweating

With the other I've been cool

Around one I act nervous

With the other I'm composed

One stole my heart

The other that is his goal

One made many promises

The other's creating his own

It's tough to decide

Which one to choose

While one's familiar territory

The other one is brand new

TODAY

It's been a month since I last saw you

And today you barely could look in my face

Even though you were smiling and talking to me

You barely could look me in the eyes

I gave you a hug

And I believe it shocked you

You returned another hug

But I could tell it was hard for you

You had me laughing a lot

I was talking a lot too

It was weird how we were

For the chemistry was true

How does one hide true love

When it's obvious we still care

Though the flesh might be weakened

The spirits remain fighting without fear

CONFUSED

Why do I feel confused?

Why do I allow myself to be so used

Why do I doubt myself

When I knew I could always help myself

I've put myself in a position

Where I've lead myself

To believe

That I could not move on without you

Why do I allow your views

To lead me to a point

Where all I ever wanted

Was to be in your shoes

A simple task it may seem

But try walking where I've been

Then tell me if that's really where

You would ever want to be

I am so confused

Yet still I continue to be used

Someday I'll get my answer

Then, it would all be worthwhile

LONG DAY

Yesterday was a very long day for me
I truly can't believe it's only been a day since we last spoke

It had been almost two weeks
Since we last laid eyes on each other

Yesterday he came by and popped in for one measly hour
An hour that only seemed like a simple minute

As quickly as it seemed he appeared here
'twas just as sudden he was gone

I had been waiting and anticipating for that moment to come
But as soon as it came, it was just as quickly gone

He flashed in like lightening
And disappeared into thin air

He left a puzzle in my mind
A feeling somewhat very rare

With a feeling of shared lost
He had me thinking things through

It all ended in utter disappointment
A feeling somewhat brand new

It seems I am always building myself up
Just to end up in the same rut

I've got to keep strong, in fact I will be strong
Actually there's no other way to be

I shall continue on my journey
The journey God has planned for me

MY APOLOGIES

Sorry babe,

I guess I was moving too fast.

What was I thinking?

When I asked you to grasp,

The way I was seeing things.

I know I am stubborn,

But can you blame a woman.

For wanting your loving arms,

Your kisses, your caress,

You've got my mind under duress.

I may have been hoping,

For a miracle,

For things to happen too soon.

I have been wondering and pondering,

I think I'm mesmerized by you.

Sorry babe,

I did not even know.

My expectations of you were too high,

I'll take it easy with you.

GOODBYE

DUMPED

Dumped!
Dropped!
Dissed!
He dogged me

You didn't even have the decency to call me

You left me hanging
Hanging without a probable cause
Without a simple explanation

You probably still want me

But how could you just leave me
It could have been so simple

But no
You had to make things seem so impossible
Just because you didn't have the guts
To face your fears

It's not as hard as you make it seem
All you had to do was say it's over
That way there would be some closure

Now I feel rotten inside
Because you didn't give me a chance
To understand the problem at hand

Because this is the easier way for you
You didn't care if it was going to be harder for me

It doesn't feel good

My first time being dissed
Forgotten like a dirty old shoe

I got dumped!
Dropped!
Dissed!

LOSER

You liar, you loser
You cold-blooded cheat
You knew there was no place
For our hearts to meet

You twisted things
To make them seem fine
You made me feel bad
With your dirty lies

You never once thought
You were hurting my heart
For you were too busy
Trying not to get caught

There was never a time
When you would have shared
There was never a time
When you really cared

You've melted my heart
You've made me feel low
You took me for granted
And for that I will go

Never was there a compliment
That came from your way
Never was there a time
That you wanted to stay

Don't bother me with excuses
Don't even try to seem fair
This woman has been around
For a number of years

Don't sugar coat things
For it's obvious you didn't care
I'll try my own way to handle
This temporary scare

REAP WHAT YOU SOW

You come to me and threaten me
With your ugly words

But how much control do you have at home?
How much do you have going on for you?
In your own life

Do you get pleasure out of stomping on me?
Does it make you happy to be so mean?

Does it make you feel powerful?
Now that you have full control
While growing old
With your unforeseen goals

It's a pity you don't know
What's in store for you
When you dish out dirt
To the ones that make you who you are today

One day will be pay day
When you will reap your reward for being so mean

DECEIVER

You lied to me!

How could you just look me in the eyes

And tell me everything was okay

You really aren't fair

It's as though you never cared

I gave you all of my trust

And just because of lust

You looked me in the eyes

And lied

I guess all you wanted

Was to take care of you and only you

Today I feel completely used

Lost inside without a clue

You deceived me

Totally betrayed my trust

All you wanted was

Well, you know what

I'm glad I didn't

Succumb to the forbidden

'twas as though God intervened

And rescued me at the most appropriate

And definitely at the most opportune time

FORGET YOU

Forget about you!

Without you I can still go on

Without you my life still has meaning

I don't know why I made myself

Believe that I would always need you

But it's not so

I still have a goal

I had one before I met you

And now I will forget you

Even though you're gone

I'm glad I made the choice to move on

Had I really stayed

I would now be swimming in tears

I DID IT

Today I did it

I made you see
How low you've made me feel

You've been so mean
When all I was trying to do
Was to be your queen

I wanted you to be my king
But you just did not understand
How to treat a woman
It seems you never had a plan

You were always the one
Who's forever acting shady
While I was only trying to be your lady

You should have never forsaken me
You should never have played me

WHAT DID YOU THINK

What was I supposed to do?

Do you think I'd always be your fool?

With all the things you put me through

Did you think I'd never have a clue?

What was I suppose to do?

Did you want me to sit here waiting?

In vain

Complaining

While maintaining this insidious relationship

Try refraining from engaging me in another

Ridiculous conversation

That has no meaning

One that's not going anywhere

But will only instead waste my time

There is no normalcy

What is that?

Do you even know

What being in a healthy relationship means?

Shhh! I don't want to hear it!

You've said enough

Now it's my turn to talk

THOUGHT I KNEW YOU

I thought I knew you
But you weren't true
I thought I knew you
But you made me blue

You've contaminated all the feelings
I'd been gathering for you
I thought I knew you
But you weren't true

Special times spent
Precious moments captured
Loving thoughts exchanged
Many emotions rendered

Our dreams we shared
My heart I surrendered
I thought we were bonding
Instead a scheme you were plotting

While you were scheming
In my heart I was beaming
Wondering if you were feeling
But instead you were cheating

Cheating me the chance
To be loved purely from your soul
Leaving me with nothing
But a chance to grow old

I thought I knew you
But you weren't true
I thought I knew you
But you made me blue

CHANGE

Why did this happen so soon

I didn't see this coming

Things were going so smooth

Until you began thinking things through

You were perfect for me

And I was perfect for you

You were the one in my dream

I was the one you said you knew

From the door you were great

Right then you gave me your heart

From then you were special

From there we were never apart

Why do these things happen to good people

We've tried everything to keep things new

We've battled all the other demons

Now this one's the hardest to chew

LIKE LIGHTENING

Like lightening you flashed in my life
Like lightening you walked out
Like lightening you left your mark
Like lightening I want you back in

Like thunder claps I've cried out loud
Like thunder you've heard my screams
Like thunder I banged on the ground
Like thunder I want you back in

Like rain my fears were washed away
Like rain my feelings were released
Like rain my spirit became dampened
Like rain I want you back in

Like floods my sorrows became overwhelming
Like floods my thoughts were in overload
Like floods my body became laden
Like the rushing of floods I want you back in

Like fire my insides were blazing
Like fire I felt the burning
Like fire I took all the heat
Like fire I want you back in

Like wind you blew out my life
Like wind my life began to spin
Like wind my world with you blew away
Like wind I want you back in

≈▲≈▲≈▲≈▲≈▲≈

DON'T GO

Please don't go now

Please don't go away

I need you right now

I need you to stay

*

I know that I've hurt you

I know I caused you pain

I'm so sorry you're leaving

So sad you couldn't stay

70

NOT AGAIN

I'm not gonna' do this

Not again

I'm not gonna' just sit here

Not again

I won't try to be there

Not again

It seems my life keeps repeating, But…

Not again

You try me and you tease me, But

Not again

You've got my head spinning, But

Not again

My heart you were hurting, But No

Not again

I won't give my full self, Oh no

Not again

WITH YOU AGAIN

The day when you told me goodbye

I thought I would never see you again

The day when you told me it's over

I just knew I would never see you again

Today you're in my life

And I'm seeing you again

It's quite a shame

That things have to be this way

Seems I've been very foolish

With you telling me what to do

I need to hang up that hat

And move on without you

TRUTH IS

Even though we're not together

Even though we can't be together

You've taught me how to love

And how to make my life much better

You've made me fall in love with you

Without even making an advance

You've made me trust and care for you

Without even knowing what was in my heart

♥†♥†♥†♥†♥†♥†♥†♥†♥

LISTEN

I'm sorry Darling.

Forget it.

You can't seem to understand where I'm coming from.

And I can't seem to understand where you're coming from.

I don't feel like dealing with this type of aggravation.

I can't handle the pain and frustration you put me through.

I don't see how you cannot see what it's like to be in my shoes.

I find it hard to comprehend what your life is possibly like.

I feel like you're shutting me out,

Before I even have a chance to get to know you.

I hardly even know you,

And already I'm getting all upset,

Over situations that I think are unnecessary.

It's unnecessary because I don't see why it is so difficult,

For you to pick up the phone,

And use common courtesy,

To explain why you can't make it.

Why is to so hard for you to see what I'm going through?

I'm not going to X out the fact that I believe,

We could make a great couple, but I cannot and will not live like this.

Good Bye!

NO ONE LIKE YOU

Never known anyone like you

Never met anyone so true

Seems to me you always knew

The perfect things to say or do

In my heart

I will always know

That you were never

Putting on a show

If only we knew

If only we'd known

That from the start

We'd fall apart

We never would try

We never would feel

It would've never existed

It would never be missed

A friendship like ours

Is out of this world

God brought us together

He put us in sync

I'm glad for the times

We have spent together

I would never trade a moment

Though the pain's hard to measure

YOU MADE ME LOVE YOU

You came into my life
At a time
When I was becoming quite comfortable
With where I was in my life

I was beginning to get used to my life
And where I stood
You blew in without a warning
Made me shy when you came calling

You stepped right in
Wined and dined me
You treated me like a lady
And you had me wondering

I wasn't quite sure
Where all of it would go
I was just waiting for an answer
And the Lord let us know

He showed us great pleasure
While rocky times acted against us
We fought without a worry
And continued to show our love

We knew there was something
Trying hard to act against us
From that we never did panic
Made us fight hard to stay together

Then there came something bigger
Than the two of us could shake
It tore us apart
It came like an earthquake

Only over time can we see
If this relationship was ever meant to be
Within our present status
Only the spirits could unleash

REALITY

TO THE CURB

After you've kicked me to the curb
Threw me in the garbage can
Pushed me down the stairs
Let me fall into the dungeon

I survived
I survived through all the storms

Even though I cried every night
With the blanket over my head
My head buried in the pillow
With my teeth grinding without end

I survived
I still survived

Though the pain was hard to bear
And the frustration had me in a slump
My spirit became weak
While my feet became numb

I survived
I truly survived

As I gazed at your photograph
There was a feeling of discontent
As I recaptured fond memories
There was a cloud hanging over my head

But I survived
I did survive

THE PLAN

It wasn't our time

It was all in His plan

God gave us His hand

Made us take a stand

He didn't want us to hurt

He just wanted us to know

How uncertain we both were

In shaping our goals

It was indeed in His plans

For all the things to unfold

He's been working while molding

And mending our souls

He gave us a rude awakening

From a shaky love we've created

He's been holding our hands

For a plan we did not understand

TOGETHER AGAIN

Today we are together again

My sorrows and pains have begun to mend

Today my life seems to make more sense

All my struggles and pains have seen the end

Seems once my life had been amiss

Only hurt and pain I knew exist

Then the day when you came, gave me a big kiss

I knew my life had all means to exist

*

I'm thankful for this life

I'm thankful for what it's revealed

I'm grateful for all the lessons

Thank God for the way I feel

♥●♥○♥●♥○♥●♥

SITUATIONS

It's funny how we sometimes go into situations, where we innocently become close to another person.

The intention was to become good buds, but for some reason the vibes seem to become a lot stronger than you can bear.

The emotions are up in the air.

Each person is in complete denial of what is happening to him/her, simply because they know it could jeopardize a friendship in the making.

Already they have a lot in common.

They share a whole lot of common interests.

They work with each other with a clear understanding of what each other may like or dislike.

They're both aware of each other's fears.

They look at each other with great intensity and they each become lost in their emotions.

It almost becomes obvious that they both are hiding something inside.

Flames of desires, and unwanted emotions have gotten them wrapped in a spider's web.

How come he always seem so attentive and he always seems to have time. He never seems too busy though he's always making up rhymes. How does she do it? She always seems fair, she's forever so beautiful and she always shows care.

He brings out something in her that she finds extremely hard to explain. Life to him is so simple. He's the example of one who takes advantage of the fact that you only live once.

CONTROL

One of the most incredible things that could ever happen to anyone in life, is falling

in love.

The funny thing is, love can come creeping up at any given time.

Love doesn't give you any warning.

It doesn't come to you slowly.

It has a way of just slapping you right in the face.

It doesn't even give one the chance to rationalize and think things over.

It is demanding and expects to be in the forefront at all times.

It takes over your heart and all the muscles in your body.

It takes full control of your thoughts.

It takes over your whole mobile process.

It brings you up to the highest high and it puts you down to the lowest lows.

It has no compassion, no care for your whole being.

It has to always come first.

It has to be the center of your being.

It can be the one thing you can trust, yet it can deceive you as well.

Love blinds you to the point where one has to question;

"Why is it that something so good for you, could be so harmful at the same time?"

SETTLE?

It seems like the only people living in life

Are the ones that settle for what they have

Right in front of them

Is this the way that it's supposed to be

Because I can't wait to be free

From this insanity

Maybe it's me that's causing the problem

Cause I can never find true happiness

If I close my eyes

Will I be set free?

Will I be wishing?

Or just lost in a dream

There's always room for fear

For we live in truth or dare

We live off hope

And the fear of not being alone

Maybe there's no such thing as reality

That's one thing I have yet to see

That is my reality.

What's your reality?

ALONE

Some people may say that it's a tragedy
Living all alone
But I know if you look inside yourself
You will be in control of what you feel

The truth will be revealed
Through all the unseen
Past events shall make sense
All hurts become real

All anger become insight
All crying will cease
More humans will be forgiven
Friends will be further appreciated

Negativity will be unacceptable
Positivism will prevail
There'll be no room for hatred
All answers become clear

So try living alone
If you haven't done so
Try experiencing all these pleasures
Tasting all the unknown

Then all the truth
Shall be revealed
And through all the invisible
Your fate you will see

REPRESSED EMOTIONS

If you keep repressing your emotions

It'll haunt you for the rest of your life

If you keep repressing your emotions

It'll haunt you until you face up to it

If you keep repressing your emotions,

It'll haunt you until you choose

To allow yourself to believe that it exists

*

The longer you wait

The more problems you face

The longer you wait

The harder for you to overcome

PEOPLE

I've come to the point where I've realized

That people will always be who they are

You just can't simply change them to who they aren't

People will sometimes do anything in their power

To deceive you without thinking

Just as long as it's in their favor

They would say whatever it takes

Anything to make themselves look good

As long as it's for their benefit

People can really try to make you look stupid

As long as it makes them look good

And assuring they will come out on top

People would stab you in the back

While smiling in your face

They could also even be quite devious

You wonder why they're speaking to you

While going around mistreating you

They tell you how they're feeling you

When in fact they wanna get rid a yah

THAT'S LIFE

People who don't know themselves,

Try to live their lives through others.

But when it doesn't work out the way they want,

They freak out and become evil.

They try to regain control by sinning,

By trying to bring down others,

While inside they're bringing down themselves,

Not realizing the damage they're causing on their own selves.

They don't realize that they are going further away,

From finding out who they truly could be.

They move further from seeing that deep down inside,

They could be an angel sent from God,

Sent down to try and finish or continue God's work.

They could even be here to help build on life's prosperity.

This is why there are only a chosen few who make it,

On becoming servants of God.

Not everyone can pass the test of God.

It is up to the individual to decide his or her own fate.

THAT'S LIFE!

UNFOLD

Visions from this condition
Is a mission to make decisions

Stipulation created by this nation
Is the foundation of our tribulations

In this world there are some of us,

Who focus on the negativities we all face.

Very few count their blessings along the way.

Many of us rely on outside gratifications,

While the rest know that true peace lies within.

There's a constant battle between good and evil,

Being young or old, being up or down.

Just simply finding a balance.

Universal forces pull us in the direction we need to go,

But we continually steer away.

We search to find the answer,

While it has always been there tapping us right on the shoulders.

We've all got to look within,

The key is locked within our souls.

Look in and the spirits shall unfold,

All the mysterious clues from the stories of old.

♪◀♪◀♪◀♪◀♪◀♪

GOD'S GIFT

There comes a time in life,

When as people we need to face reality.

We need to accept what's given to us,

Which is the one sure thing we have.

That given thing is truth.

The beauty of life is,

God has given us the ability,

To sense or feel whenever something isn't right.

We always deep down inside know or sense,

When we are out of sync with the universe.

Our common strife is to always be in control,

Yet we cannot see that we are the opponents of ourselves.

In life there will always be crossroads,

But there will never be one too hard to bear.

It will always seem like the most difficult task,

But in reality it's the truth we need to face.

Not very often in life do people find someone,

Who can make them feel complete.

It is not easy for one to find true love.

However if that is causing grief upon another,

There is no way that you should be a part of it

What goes around comes around.